I0818546

WNBA
LOS ANGELES SPARKS
Mitchell Lane
PUBLISHERS
Kerry Kelaher Fredeen

Mitchell Lane

PUBLISHERS

mitchelllanepub.com

2001 SW 31st Avenue
Hallandale, FL 33009

First Edition, 2026.
Author: Kerry Kelaher Fredeen
Designer: Ed Morgan
Editor: Tammy Gagne

Series: WNBA
Title: Los Angeles Sparks

Library bound ISBN: 979-8-89260-481-9
eBook ISBN: 979-8-89260-491-8

Photo credits: p. 5, 7, 9 newscom.com; p. 11 sportslogos.net; p. 15 wikimedia; balance Alamy

CONTENTS

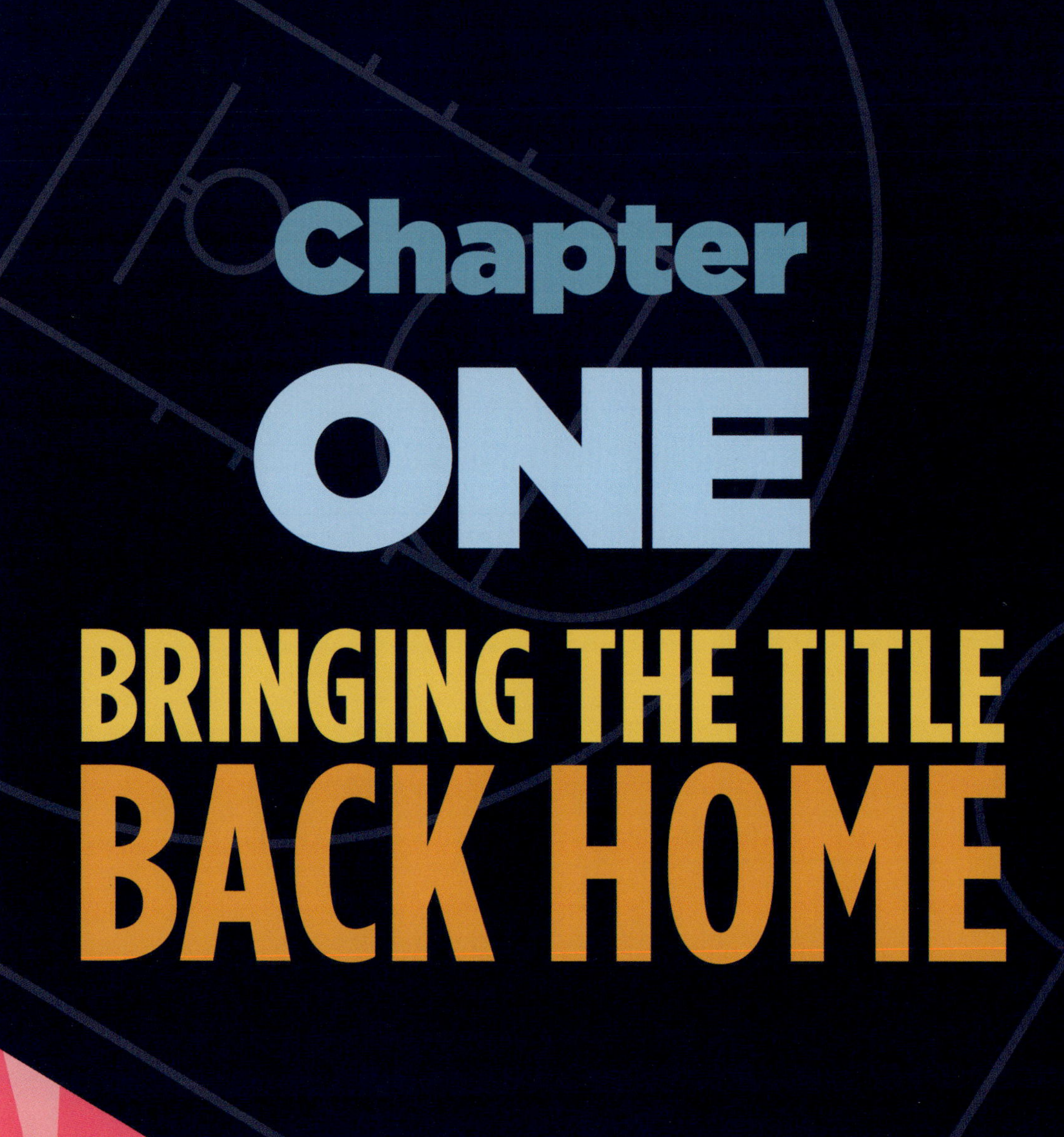

Chapter ONE

BRINGING THE TITLE BACK HOME

Forward Nneka Ogwumike grabs a rebound from Lynx center Sylvia Fowles in game five of the 2016 WNBA Finals.

It was game five of the 2016 WNBA Finals. On October 20, the two top teams in the league, the Los Angeles (L.A.) Sparks and the Minnesota Lynx, were facing off in Minneapolis. The Lynx were the current champions and looking to hold onto the title. The Sparks were coming off two losing seasons.

CHAPTER ONE

The Sparks were back-to-back champs in 2001 and 2002. They wanted to bring the trophy back to Los Angeles. But they were facing a tough opponent in the Lynx, who led the league with a 28–6 record.

The best-of-five series was tied at two games each. Game five was a close one from the beginning. The lead changed eleven times in the first half.

It all came down to the final seconds. The Lynx's Rebekkah Brunson made one of two free throws with 23.4 seconds left to give her team a 74–73 lead. Sparks veteran Candace Parker scored, but she was matched by the Lynx's Maya Moore. Then with only seconds remaining, the Sparks' Nneka Ogwumike got the ball. Her first attempt was blocked, but she grabbed the rebound and finished what she started. The Sparks were bringing the title back to Los Angeles after fourteen years.

Bringing the Title Back Home

Lisa Leslie holds the WNBA Championship trophy as the Sparks celebrate their victory over the Charlotte Sting in the 2001 Finals.

FAST FACT

In 2001, the Sparks became the first WNBA team to go undefeated at home for a whole season.

CHAPTER ONE

Parker summed up the experience to ESPN. "The journey to get here, I wouldn't have wanted to do it with anybody else. It's amazing, when you surround yourself with good people, how fun it is."

The Sparks were one of the original eight WNBA teams. They are one of only three teams that are still playing in their original cities. They've had ups and downs since the beginning, but their talent and dedication have made them a **legacy** in women's basketball.

Bringing the Title Back Home

The Los Angeles Sparks celebrate after defeating the Minnesota Lynx for the WNBA Championship on October 20, 2016.

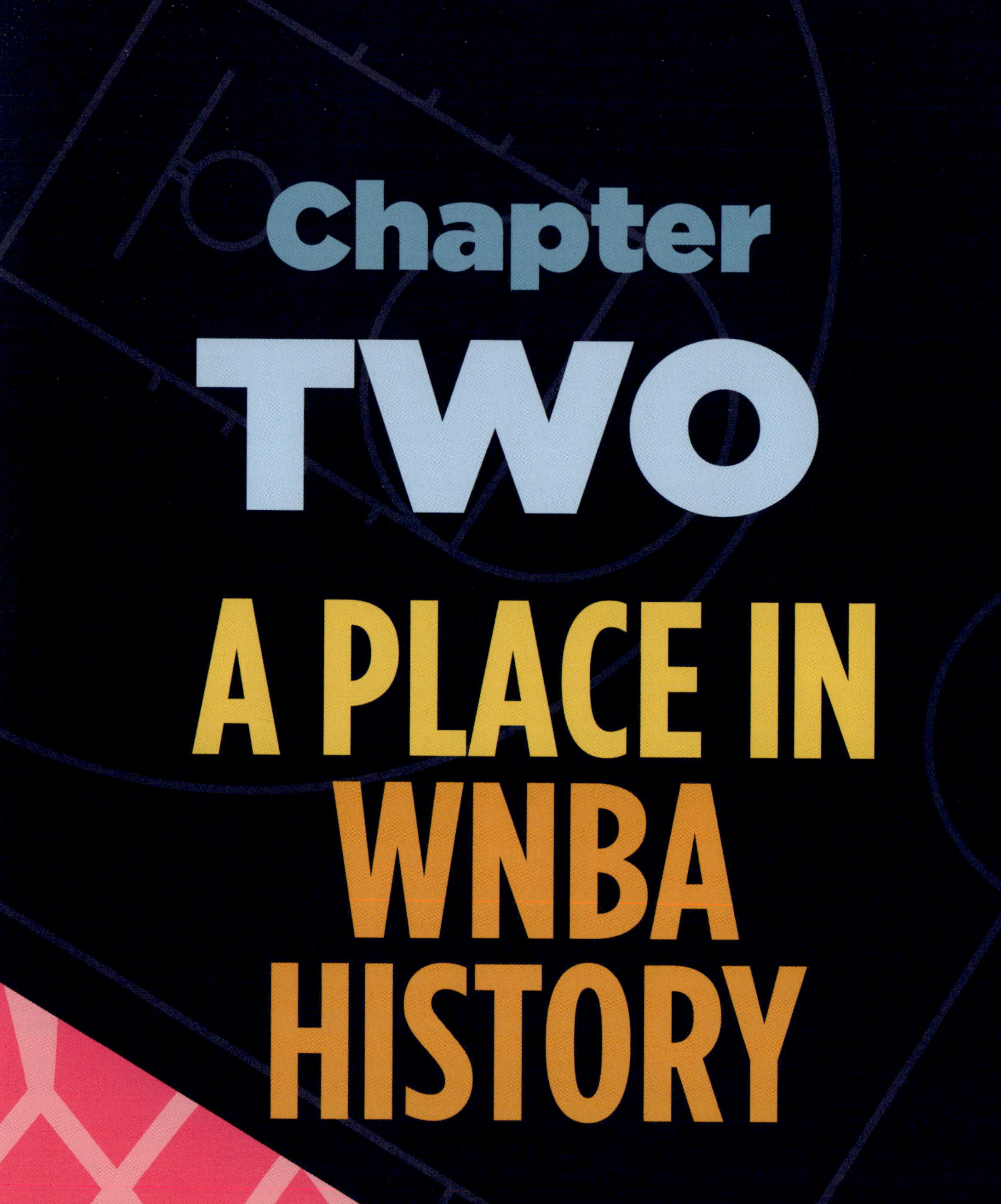

Chapter TWO

A PLACE IN WNBA HISTORY

Sparks logo 1997–2020

The Sparks began making history from the start. The first-ever WNBA game was held in Inglewood, California, on June 21, 1997. It featured the Sparks versus the New York Liberty. The Sparks' Penny Toler scored the first basket in a WNBA game. Looking back on the moment, Toler told ESPN "I might have only slept two or three hours the night before, because of the excitement. I was just hoping not to be tired at **tipoff**. But I think my energy came on because I knew something incredible was happening right now."

CHAPTER TWO

The Sparks won their first championship four years later, beating the Charlotte Sting in the 2001 WNBA Finals. In 2002, Los Angeles became the second team in league history to score back-to-back championships with a win over the New York Liberty. The first team to manage this feat was the Houston Comets, who stopped playing after the 2008 season. The Sparks were the first WNBA team to have a perfect record in their playoff run, with 6–0.

A Place in WNBA History

The Los Angeles Sparks' Lisa Leslie, (right), tries to grab a rebound from the Phoenix Mercury's Jennifer Lacy.

FAST FACT

The Los Angeles Sparks are one of only three remaining original WNBA teams. The other two are the New York Liberty and the Phoenix Mercury.

CHAPTER TWO

Los Angeles has long been known for its success in basketball. The city is also home to the Lakers, one of the top teams in the National Basketball Association (NBA). And the Sparks have given L.A. sports fans another reason to cheer. With playoff appearances in the double digits and three championships, the Sparks are among the **franchises** with the most wins in WNBA history.

The city of Los Angeles has **embraced** the Sparks, and the team gives back to the community. The Jr. Sparks program holds clinics, camps, and tournaments for young girls, many of whom are inspired by the professional athletes. The Jr. Sparks also host **coed** camps and clinics to "allow boys and girls to train together as athletes and experience positive social relationships."

A Place in WNBA History

Crystal Dangerfield signed with the Sparks in 2024.

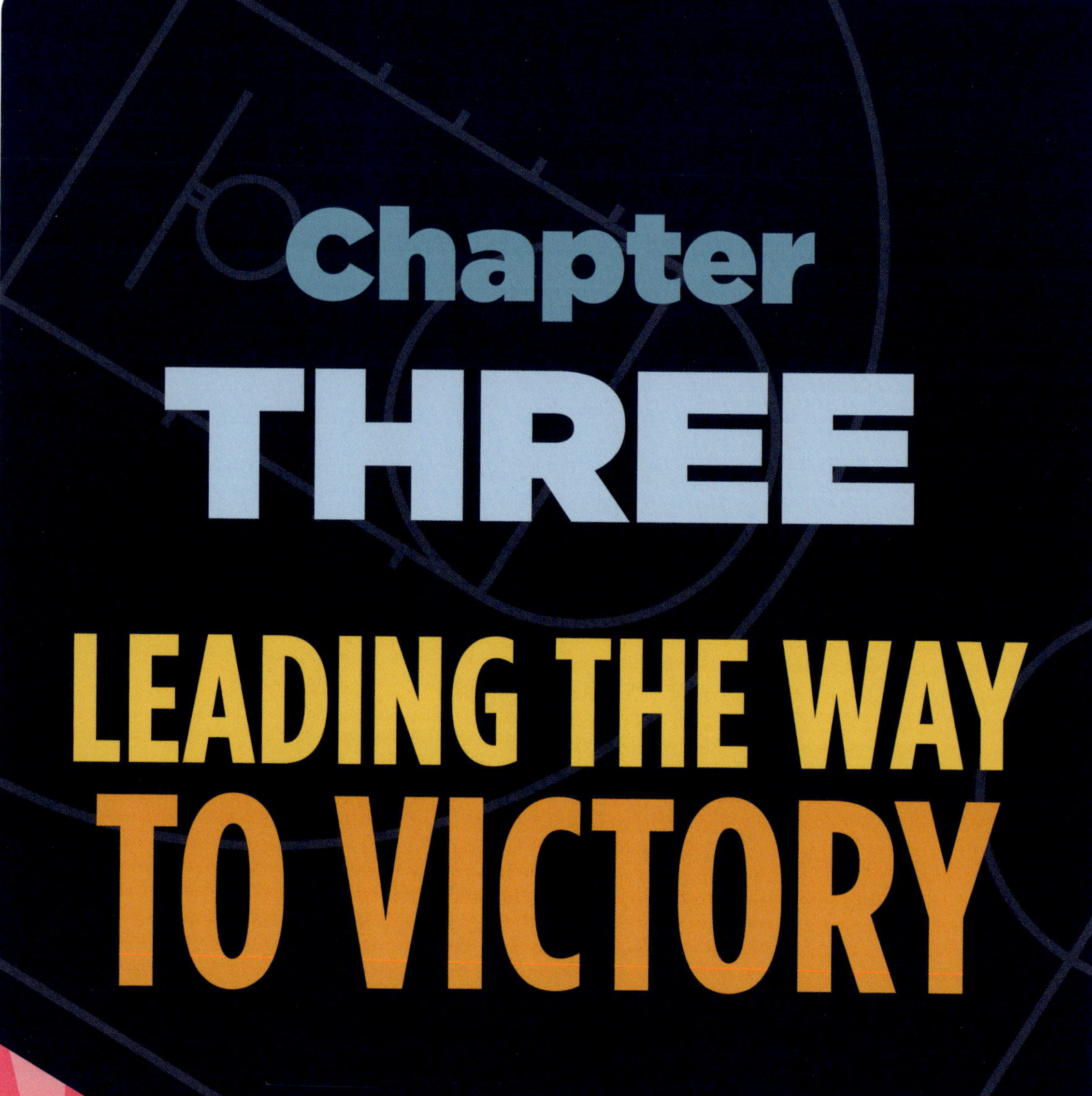

Chapter THREE

LEADING THE WAY TO VICTORY

Zia Cook of the Sparks drives to the basket during a game against the Chicago Sky.

With their long history, the Sparks have seen many changes over the years. In addition to players being drafted or traded, many different people have coached the team. The Sparks have had sixteen head coaches since 1997.

CHAPTER THREE

The most successful coach was Michael Cooper. He guided the team for eight seasons. Under his watch, the Sparks had a 167–85 record. He led them to its championships in 2001 and 2002.

When Carol Ross was named head coach in 2012, the team was coming back from a challenging year. Ross helped the Sparks make it to the playoffs again. For that, she was named WNBA Coach of the Year.

Curt Miller became the Sparks head coach in 2023. He came to Los Angeles after seven years with the Connecticut Sun, a team he led to the finals twice. Miller was a two-time Coach of the Year with the Sun, but he was excited to begin his new role with the Sparks.

Leading the Way to Victory

Forwards Rickea Jackson (left) and Cameron Brink (right) with Curt Miller

FAST FACT

On August 6, 2023, Curt Miller had his 150th WNBA win in a Sparks game against the Washington Mystics.

Miller told ESPN "L.A. holds a special place in my heart, and I always said if I had an opportunity at some point in my career to lead this **iconic** franchise, it would be hard to pass up." In addition to taking over the Sparks, Miller was named a scout for the USA women's basketball team for the 2024 Paris Olympics. He left the Sparks at the end of 2024.

Lynne Roberts took over as the team's head coach following Miller's departure. She had previously been the head coach for the University of Utah. Under her leadership, the Utes made it into the NCAA Tournament playoffs three times.

Leading the Way to Victory

Lynne Roberts expressed hopes of making the Los Angeles Sparks the top WNBA team when she was named the new head coach in 2024.

Chapter FOUR

LEGENDS AND STARS

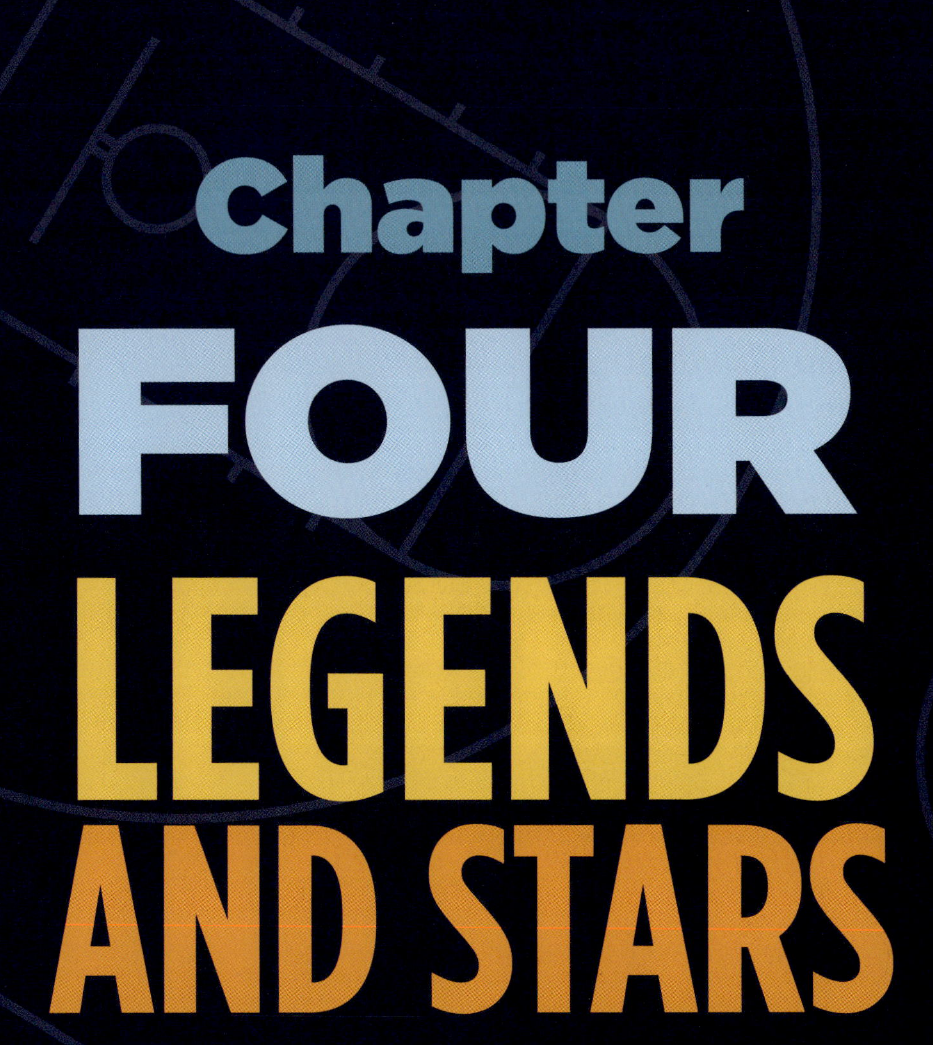

Lisa Leslie hoists the 2002 All-Star MVP trophy.

One of the first players the Sparks signed was **center** Lisa Leslie. She was National College Player of the Year in 1994. Leslie was already an Olympic gold medalist when she joined the Sparks. She was also the first WNBA player to win the title of Most Valuable Player (MVP) for the regular season, All-Star Game MVP, and playoff MVP in the same season. And she led the team to back-to-back titles in 2001 and 2002. Leslie spent her entire WNBA career with the Sparks before retiring in 2009.

CHAPTER FOUR

Forward Dearica Hamby joined the Sparks in 2023. She was traded from the Las Vegas Aces, where she helped that team win the 2022 championship. Hamby was also a two-time All-Star with the Aces. In her first years with the Sparks, Hamby's experience was valuable to a team that was rebuilding its **roster**. Coach Curt Miller told the *Los Angeles Times*. "[Hamby] is leading in her role . . . and she's leading by example. She's teaching our young players how hard it is to win in this league." And in 2024, she was part of Team USA at the Paris Olympics, where she took home a bronze medal in women's 3x3 basketball. Also called 3-on-3, this is a fast-paced version of the sport with just three players on each team.

Dearica Hamby won a medal for Team USA at the 2024 Paris Olympics.

FAST FACT

Sparks sent four players to the 2024 Olympics in Paris. They played for four different countries: the United States, Australia, Canada, and China.

CHAPTER FOUR

Guard Aari McDonald is one of the newest members of the Sparks. She joined the team in 2024, after three seasons with the Atlanta Dream. She was named to the WNBA All-**Rookie** Team in 2021. This honor is given to the top five rookie players in the league each year. McDonald is fast and a dependable shooter who found her place in Los Angeles. She went from being a bench player with the Dream to a starter with the Sparks.

Los Angeles focused largely on rebuilding the team in 2024, and McDonald's drive and skills were part of that vision. When McDonald signed with the team, Coach Miller said, "Over her WNBA career [McDonald] has shown herself to be one of the fastest guards in the league." Miller is confident that she will help the team keep winning.

The Sparks have built a legacy in the WNBA. They have brought championships to Los Angeles. They have an eye on the future, and they are looking forward to bringing more titles home.

Legends and Stars

Guard Aari McDonald fights off Lynx forwards Bridget Carleton (back left) and Alanna Smith (right) during a game in Minnesota.

GLOSSARY

center
A basketball player who plays near the basket, often the tallest member of the team

coed
Relating to both male and female participants

embraced
Accepted enthusiastically

forward
A basketball player who plays near the basket, often rebounding and scoring points

franchises
Teams in a professional sports league

guard
A basketball player who focuses on passing, dribbling, and setting up plays

iconic
Well established and widely recognized

legacy
A person or group with a longstanding history of success

rookie
An athlete playing her first season as a member of a professional sports team

roster
A list of players on a sports team

tipoff
The act in which two opposing centers jump to take possession of the ball at the beginning of a basketball game

SLAM DUNK WNBA TRIVIA

- The Sparks play at the Crypto.com Arena in downtown Los Angeles.
- The Sparks mascot is Sparky, a dancing dog.
- The Sparks' main colors are purple and gold. These are the same colors worn by their NBA counterparts, the Los Angeles Lakers.
- In 2003, Lisa Leslie became the first WNBA player to dunk a ball in a game.
- NBA legend Magic Johnson is an owner of the Sparks.
- Despite their long history of great players, the Sparks have only retired two jerseys, Lisa Leslie's number 9 and Penny Toler's number 11.

FIND OUT MORE

IN PRINT

Chandler, Matt. *Basketball Biographies for Kids: The Greatest NBA and WNBA Players from the 1960s to Today*. Callisto Kids, 2022.

Helt, Julianna. *Minnesota Lynx*. Mitchell Lane Publishers, 2026.

Rule, Heather. *Candace Parker*. Focus Readers, 2022.

ON THE INTERNET

Los Angeles Sparks.
https://sparks.wnba.com.

"Los Angeles Sparks," *ESPN*, n.d.
www.espn.com/wnba/team/_/name/la/los-angeles-sparks.

"Los Angeles Sparks," *FOX Sports*, n.d.
www.foxsports.com/wnba/los-angeles-sparks-team.

INDEX

About the Author

Kerry Kelaher Fredeen lives in Hollywood, California. She has written several books for young readers. When she's not busy writing, she works at a Southern California library. Her love of sports began as a child, watching games with her dad in New Jersey.